REMAINS TO BE SEEN

EXPLORING THE AZTECS

REMAINS TO BE SEEN

EXPLORING THE AZTECS

JOHN MALAM

EVANS BROTHERS LIMITED

First published in paperback in 2003
Evans Brothers Limited
2A Portman Mansions
Chiltern Street
London W1U 6NR

Reprinted 2005

This book is based on *Indiana Jones Explores The Aztecs*, first published in 1994

Printed in Grafo, S.A. Basauri

ISBN 0 237 525984

British Library Cataloguing in Publication data.
A catalogue record for this book is available from the British Library.

Acknowledgements

The author and publishers would like to thank the following people for their valuable help and advice:

Dr Anne Miilard BA (Hons) Dip. ed., Dip Arc., Ph.D. author, archaeologist and lecturer

Illustrations: Virginia Gray
Maps: Jillie Luff, Bitmap Graphics

Editor Jean Coppendale
Design: Neil Sayer
Production: Jenny Mulvanny

For permission to reproduce copyright material the author and publishers gratefully acknowledge the following:

Cover photograph: Temples at Chichen Itza, e.t. archive

Title page: ceremonial mask inlaid with mosaic of turquoise and shell, British Museum

page 8 ZEFA **page 9** ZEFA **page 10** (top) Anthropology Museum, Veracruz University, Jalapa, Werner Forman Archive, (bottom) Dr John B Free, Heritage and Natural History Photography **page 11** (middle left) ZEFA, (middle right) University of Essex, Trip, (bottom) Dr John B Free, Heritage and Natural History Photography **page 12** AKG/Image Select **page 13** The Bodleain Library **page 14** Werner Forman Archive **page 16** (top) Tony Morrison, South American Pictures, (bottom) The Bodleain Library **page 18** (top) CM Dixon, (bottom) The Bodleain Library **page 19** The Bodleain Library **page 20** (top) Museum fur Volkerkunde, (bottom) AKG/Image Select **page 21** e.t. archive **page 22** The Bodleain Library **page 23** National Museum of Anthropology, Mexico City, Werner Forman Archive **page 24** (middle) Dr John B Free, Heritage and Natural History Photography, (bottom) The Bodleain Library **page 25** British Museum **page 26** (left) Ted Stephan, Cephas Picture Library, (right) Dr John B Free, Heritage and Natural History Photography **page 27** (top) The Bodleain Library, (bottom) CM Dixon **page 28** (top) AKG/Image Select, (bottom) Ancient Art and Architecture Collection **page 29** (top left) British Museum, Werner Forman Archive, (middle) British Museum, The Bridgeman Art Library, (bottom) Ancient Art and Architecture Collection **page 31** (top) Liverpool Museum, Werner Forman Archive, (bottom) British Museum, The Bridgeman Art Library **page 32** (left) Wurttembergisches Landesmuseum Stuttgart, Robert Harding Picture Library, (right) University of Essex, Trip **page 33** (top) British Museum, (bottom) British Museum, Werner Forman Archive **page 34** (top) British Museum, Werner Forman Archive, (bottom) British Museum, Werner Forman Archive **page 35** (top left) Robert Frerck, Robert Harding Picture Library, (top right) Dr John B Free, Heritage and Natural History Photography, (bottom) e.t. archive **page 36** (left) ZEFA, (right) CM Dixon **page 40** (left) British Museum, Werner Forman Archive, (right) The Hutchison Library **page 41** (top left) British Museum, (top right) Nick Saunders, Barbara Heller Photo Library, (bottom) e.t. archive **page 42** Giraudon, The Bridgeman Art Library **page 43** (top) Biblioteca Nacional, Madrid, The Bridgeman Art Library, (bottom left)Ancient Art and Architecture Collection, (bottom right) Bilbioteca Nacional, Madrid, The Bridgeman Art Library **page 44** (top) ZEFA, (bottom) Robert Frerck, Robert Harding Picture Library **page 45** (left) CC Lockwood, Bruce Coleman Ltd, (right) Dr John B Free, Heritage and Natural History Photography

Contents

TIMELINE OF THE AZTECS
and the rest of the world

WORLD HISTORY		AZTEC HISTORY	
1200	Rise of the Inca Empire in Peru	1200	The nomadic Aztec tribe reached the Valley of Mexico claiming to be descendants of the warlike Toltecs
1200s	Rise of the Mongol Empire in Asia and Europe		
		1200 to 1300	The Aztecs moved up and down the Valley of Mexico in search of their own land
1271–95	Marco Polo travelled to China		
1300s	Great Zimbabwe city built in Africa	1325	The traditional date when the Aztecs are said to have settled on an island in Lake Texcoco
1347–53	Black Death plague in Europe		
		1350 to 1400	The Aztecs built their island capital of Tenochtitlan and conquered tribes throughout the Valley of Mexico
1492	Christopher Columbus sailed to the 'New World' (America)	1400 to 1500	The Aztecs became the strongest tribe in the Valley of Mexico
1510	The first slaves from Africa were taken to America	1502 to 1520	Reign of Moctezuma II, the last great Aztec Emperor
		August 1519	A small Spanish army, led by Hernán Cortés, arrived in Mexico
		November 1519	Cortés met Moctezuma at Tenochtitlan. The Aztecs treated the Spaniards as gods. The Spaniards took Moctezuma prisoner
1520	Magellan sailed across the Pacific Ocean	May to July 1520	An Aztec uprising almost defeated the Spaniards. Moctezuma was killed in the fighting
1520s	The potato was introduced to Europe from South America		
1532	Spaniards made contact with the Incas of Peru, led by Francisco Pizarro. Their empire was looted and destroyed	1521	Cortés returned to Tenochtitlan with a large army of Indians opposed to the Aztecs. Disease had killed many of the Aztecs in the city, and after a great battle the Aztecs were defeated. Tenochtitlan was destroyed and the Aztec Empire broke up
		1547	Cortés died in Spain
1550s	Tobacco was introduced to Europe from South America	1567	Cortés's body was returned to Mexico and buried in the cathedral built from the stones of the Aztecs' Great Temple
1588	The Spanish Armada was defeated by an English fleet		
		1970s	Remains of the Aztecs' Great Temple uncovered by archaeologists

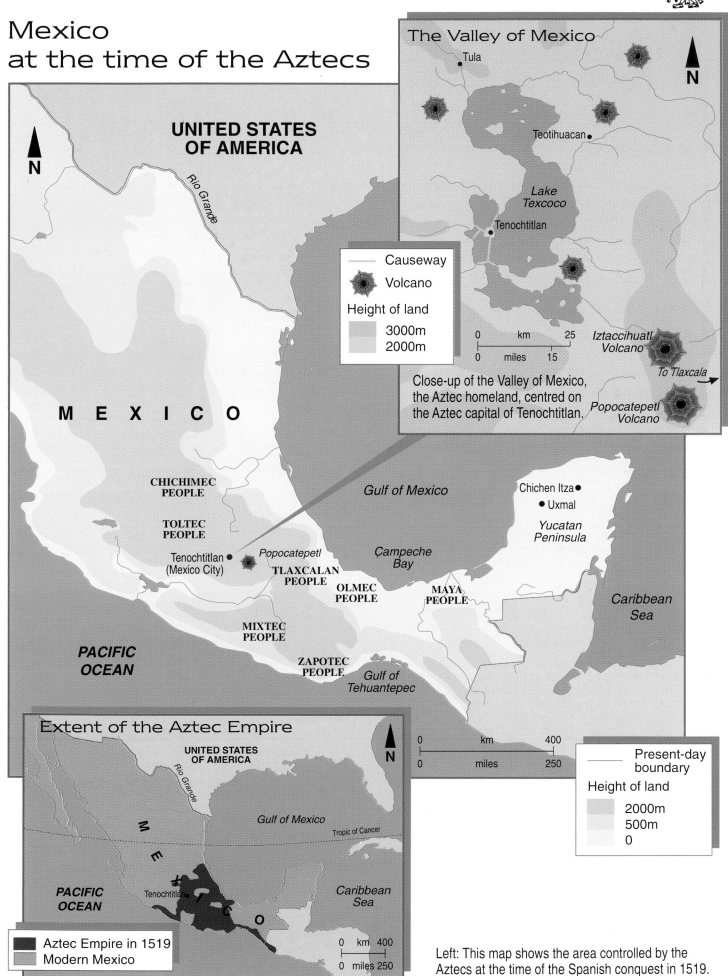

Mexico at the time of the Aztecs

UNITED STATES OF AMERICA

N

Rio Grande

M E X I C O

The Valley of Mexico

N

Tula

Teotihuacan

Lake Texcoco

Tenochtitlan

Causeway

Volcano

Height of land

3000m

2000m

0   km   25

0   miles   15

Iztaccihuatl Volcano

To Tlaxcala

Popocatepetl Volcano

Close-up of the Valley of Mexico, the Aztec homeland, centred on the Aztec capital of Tenochtitlan.

CHICHIMEC PEOPLE

TOLTEC PEOPLE

Gulf of Mexico

Chichen Itza

Uxmal

Yucatan Peninsula

Tenochtitlan (Mexico City)

Popocatepetl

TLAXCALAN PEOPLE

OLMEC PEOPLE

Campeche Bay

MAYA PEOPLE

Caribbean Sea

MIXTEC PEOPLE

ZAPOTEC PEOPLE

Gulf of Tehuantepec

PACIFIC OCEAN

0   km   400

0   miles   250

Present-day boundary

Height of land

2000m

500m

0

Extent of the Aztec Empire

N

UNITED STATES OF AMERICA

Rio Grande

M E X I C O

Gulf of Mexico

Tropic of Cancer

PACIFIC OCEAN

Tenochtitlan

Caribbean Sea

Aztec Empire in 1519

Modern Mexico

0   km   400

0   miles   250

Left: This map shows the area controlled by the Aztecs at the time of the Spanish conquest in 1519.

7

WHO WERE THE AZTECS?

Introduction to the Aztecs

The Aztecs were one of the greatest native civilizations of South America. Their homeland, which was in the present-day country of Mexico, was centred on the fertile Valley of Mexico. To begin with, they were little more than a minor group of people who had wandered into the valley in search of a suitable place to live. Other peoples already lived in the area, and the only land available to the new arrivals was an island in the middle of Lake Texcoco. It was there that the Aztecs founded their capital city of Tenochtitlan, in about 1325. During the course of the next 100 years the Aztecs increased in strength and prosperity, and by the 1420s they had emerged as the most powerful group in the Valley of Mexico. By the early 1500s they had expanded their territory and gained control of a large part of Central America.

Aztec society was based on farming and fighting – farmers produced food to feed the people and warriors defeated neighbouring tribes. But they were skilled at crafts, too. Sculptors and potters produced magnificent works of art from stone and clay, and painters recorded valuable information about the Aztec world in books.

Popocatepetl, whose name means the Smoking Mountain, is an active volcano that dominates the Valley of Mexico. At 5,456 metres high it is the second highest mountain in Mexico. Spanish soldiers who invaded the Aztec kingdom in the 1500s made gunpowder with sulphur collected from Popocatepetl's smoking crater.

Hernán Cortés, the leader of an invading Spanish army in the 1500s (see page 42), destroyed the Aztec capital of Tenochtitlan. He proclaimed that, "the new city of Mexico shall be built upon the ashes of Tenochtitlan, and as it was the principal and ruling city of all these provinces, so shall it be from this time forward." His wishes have come true, and today Mexico City is a vast, sprawling centre of over eight million people.

Mexico had been occupied by many different groups of people for thousands of years before the arrival of the Aztecs. Each group had its own identity and to the trained eye of an archaeologist the differences between them are clear to see.

Compared with the Ancient Egyptians who lived 5,000 years ago and the Ancient Greeks of 2,500 years ago, the Aztecs were really modern by our standards of time. They flourished only 600 years ago, or to put it another way, about 20 generations of people ago! The Aztec civilization was short-lived and lasted for only about 200 years. It might have lasted longer had it not been for the arrival of Europeans in the early 1500s – their coming brought the Aztec world to a speedy and tragic end.

Fact File

Mexico – land of the Aztecs

Mexico is a large country in Central America. It has a varied landscape with deserts, jungles, plains and mountains. There are almost 10,000 kilometres of coastline, and offshore are coral reefs. At the heart of the country is the Valley of Mexico – the homeland of several ancient civilizations. The Valley is at high altitude (about 2,100 metres above sea level) and is about 120 kilometres long and 65 kilometres wide. It is surrounded by mountains and at one end are the snow-capped volcanoes of Popocatepetl ('Smoking Mountain') and Itaccihuatl ('White Lady'). The Valley of Mexico became the centre of the Aztec world, and Tenochtitlan, their capital, became the site of Mexico City, the modern capital. The Aztecs called their land 'Anahuac' which meant the 'land on the edge of the waters'.

Mexico before the Aztecs

Many different groups of people lived in Mexico before the arrival of the Aztecs. The civilization of the Aztecs was based on older ones developed by earlier societies, some of which are described here.

Olmecs (1200 to 400 BC)

The Olmecs were the first civilization of Mexico. Their influence over later civilizations was so strong that they have been called Mexico's 'mother culture'. They seem to have been warlike because they made carvings of heavily armed warriors. They traded for rare stones such as obsidian and jade from which they carved figures of gods and animals such as the jaguar.

Teotihuacan (100 BC to AD 750)

This was the first great city in Mexico – but we do not know which people lived there. The Aztecs called it the 'city of the gods'. Teotihuacan may have had 200,000 inhabitants, making it the largest city in the world at the time. Its streets were built to a grid-pattern and were lined with temple pyramids. The city lay on an important trade route, and it had control over the supply of obsidian – a much-prized glassy volcanic rock used to make weapons and ornaments. It was for these reasons that Teotihuacan grew into a major urban centre. However, by AD 750 the city lay in ruins, perhaps because it was invaded by nomadic groups of people, or maybe it was deserted when the climate became drier and crops failed in the fields.

A massive stone head carved by the Olmecs. It is nearly 3 metres high and may represent one of their rulers, but his name is not known. Note how his ear-lobe is pierced and stretched. The wearing of ear ornaments was widely practised amongst the peoples of ancient Central and South America. Many giant heads carved by the Olmecs have so far been discovered. Traces of paint show that they were brightly decorated.

Teotihuacan, the city built by a mysterious and unknown people. At its centre were the great step-pyramids of the sun and moon gods. To give you an idea of how big this pyramid is, look for the people standing at the top of it.

Toltecs (AD 900 to 1150)

Toltecs, whose name means 'artists', were the last of the great civilizations before the Aztecs. They were a military people who took over styles of art and building from the people they conquered. From Tula, their capital, they governed their empire by force.

Maya (300 BC to AD 1500)

The civilization of the Maya overlapped with that of the Aztecs. The Maya were a sophisticated people who built grand cities. They used a system of picture writing that has only recently been understood.

These stone columns, which are 4 metres high, are at the Toltec capital of Tula. They once held up the roof of a temple dedicated to Quetzalcoatl, the Wind God. This god was worshipped by other people (including the Aztecs), not just the Toltecs. The columns have been carved to look like Toltec people.

Aztecs enter the Valley of Mexico

The Aztecs first entered the Valley of Mexico in about 1200, arriving as a tribe of nomads from a mysterious place in the north of the country called Aztlan, from where the name Aztec comes. At this time the Valley was already heavily populated and there was little land left for the Aztecs. An Aztec story had said their tribe would eventually settle at a place where an eagle on a cactus plant would be seen. In about 1325 this sign appeared on a swampy island in Lake Texcoco. The Aztecs settled on the island and began to build their city of Tenochtitlan, whose name means 'place of the prickly pear cactus' (also see page 14).

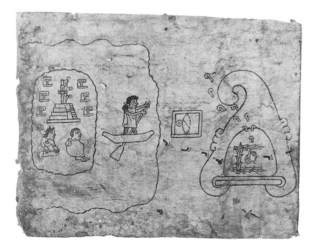

An Aztec drawing showing the migration route taken by the Aztecs. Aztlan, their island homeland, is shown on the left. After crossing a lake by canoe, footprints mark the way to a cave in a mountain, where a god gave directions which told the tribe to continue travelling south towards the Valley of Mexico.

The Maya were skilled at cutting and shaping stone for building. This temple is at the Maya city of Chichen Itza, in the far east of Mexico.

THE EMPIRE OF THE AZTECS

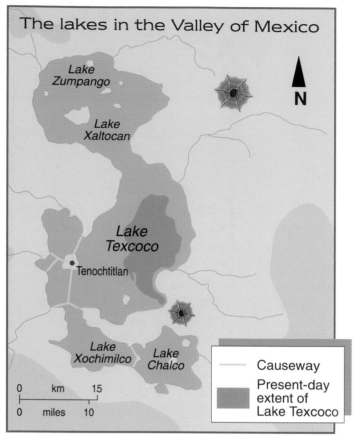

The lakes in the Valley of Mexico

Lake Zumpango

Lake Xaltocan

Lake Texcoco

Tenochtitlan

N

Lake Xochimilco

Lake Chalco

0   km   15

0   miles   10

Causeway

Present-day extent of Lake Texcoco

At the time the Aztecs settled on their island in Lake Texcoco there were five connected lakes in the Valley of Mexico. Today, the lakes have nearly disappeared as Mexico City has expanded and drained their shallow waters.

Starting the empire

The Aztecs were newcomers to the Valley of Mexico and at first they had no land of their own. Other groups of people already lived in the Valley, and they had claimed the best land. For about 100 years the Aztecs wandered up and down the Valley working for the people who were already living there. You can think of early Aztecs as an unpopular tribe struggling to survive. Eventually, the Aztecs were allowed to live on an island in Lake Texcoco because it was of no use to anyone else: it had poor, wet soil and little timber. Despite this, the Aztecs settled there. But far from being a poor place to live, the island had good points which the Aztecs used to their advantage. Because it was an island it was hard to attack but easy to defend. It was near to the kingdoms of other groups in the Valley and it became a jumping off point for making conquests. The island became a safe place to live.

The Aztecs grew in strength and formed a partnership with other tribes. Between them they ruled the Valley of Mexico and far beyond. When the Aztecs became the strongest tribe they claimed the land as theirs and ruled the other tribes. From the regions they conquered they obtained timber and food. The conquered tribes supplied them with jade, gold, rubber and slaves. The Aztecs became wealthy and could afford to turn Tenochtitlan into a fabulous capital city.

The Aztecs took ideas from other tribes, especially the Toltecs from whom they said they were descended. This stone figure is called a 'chacmool'. In its hands is a dish which was used to hold blood and other offerings to the gods. Figures such as this were first made by the Toltecs and copied later by the Aztecs.

Fact File

Kidnapping history

History can be used in many different ways. In the wrong hands history can be used like a weapon, turning people against others because the history-teller does not tell the truth. It seems that the Aztecs realized how important history could be for them and that they could turn it to their advantage. When they became the dominant people in the Valley of Mexico they began to claim they were descended from the Toltecs (see page 11). They robbed the Toltec capital of Tula and stripped it of whatever they wanted for their own capital of Tenochtitlan, 75 kilometres to the south. We know the Aztecs were not really connected with the mighty Toltecs – but imagine how powerful it must have made the Aztecs seem when they began spreading this story amongst the tribes around them.

The Aztecs believed an eagle in a cactus bush was the sign that would show them where they would eventually settle. The sign appeared in about 1325, the traditional date for the founding of their capital Tenochtitlan. This illustration was made by an Aztec artist in the 1500s. It shows the city's founders seated around the eagle. Today, a similar eagle design is used on Mexico's national flag.

Tenochtitlan – city on a lake

Fact File

Farming the land

How did the Aztecs succeed as farmers if their overcrowded island had so little land? They drained the swamps which surrounded Tenochtitlan to reclaim land for farming. Then they turned it into fertile strips called 'chinampas' or floating gardens, some of which are still in use today. The boggy land was divided up and each strip was separated from its neighbour by a canal. Plants and fertile mud from the lake were heaped on to the strips, the sides of which were supported by posts. More layers were added until the strip was above the water level. Fast-growing willow trees, whose roots anchored the new land to the lake-bed, were planted at the corners. Fertilized with human waste collected from homes within the city, and with a plentiful supply of water, up to seven crops a year could be grown and harvested.

Farming tools were very simple. A digging stick was used to dig trenches for seeds and plants.

The island on which Tenochtitlan, the Aztecs' capital city, stood was connected to the mainland by three causeways (raised paths) made of volcanic rock, earth and stone. Canals were the main routes in the city – six major canals ran north to south and two went from east to west. There were many minor canals, too. Thousands of canoes transported people, animals and other goods along the city's watery roads. The Aztecs had no wheeled transport and to have an efficient water transport system was very important.

At the centre of the city was a massive walled square, its boggy surface made hard with rocks and earth. Here were temples to the gods. Outside the square was the palace of the ruler, from where the Aztec empire was governed. It was a large building with many rooms, gardens, courtyards and even a bird-house and a zoo!

As Tenochtitlan grew into the richest and most powerful city in the whole of the Americas, more and more people were attracted to it. With little firm ground to build on, the Aztecs set about solving the problem of land shortage by creating artificial islands linked by canals. They rammed wooden posts into the shallow water and tipped rocks and earth over them as foundations for new buildings. At its peak the city may have had a population of 250,000 lake-dwellers.

Remains of the Aztecs' 'floating gardens' can still be seen in Mexico City. Trees have been planted along the edge of each plot of land. The trees' roots help to fix the floating land to the lake-bed.

Seen from the mainland, Tenochtitlan presented an amazing sight to visitors. This illustration is set in the year 1519, the year the Aztec capital was first seen by Spaniards. Lake Texcoco surrounded the island on which Tenochtitlan was built. Causeways (raised paths) linked it to the shore and at its heart was a temple complex. At the edges of the island were the 'chinampas' or floating gardens and between them were the canals that acted as the city's network of roads. On seeing the city for the first time, Bernal Díaz, a Spanish soldier, said, "It was all so wonderful...this first glimpse of things never heard of, seen or dreamed before."

The people – nobles and commoners

The maguey cactus was much used by the Aztecs. Its juice was fermented to make a mildly alcoholic drink called 'pulque'. Its dried leaves were used as fuel and for thatching and its spines became sewing needles. The long fibres from its leaves were woven into coarse, linen-like cloth.

The Aztec emperors

Name (dates of reign)
Acamapichtli (1375–1395)
Huitzilihuitl (1395–1417)
Chimalpopoca (1417–1426)
Itzcoatl (1427–1440)
Moctezuma I (1440–1469)
Axayacatl (1469–1481)
Tizoc (1481–1486)
Ahuitzotl (1486–1502)
Moctezuma II (1502–1520)
Cuitlahuac (1520)
Cuauhtemoc (1520–1525)

Aztec people were short and stocky in appearence. Men were about 1m 67cm (5ft 6in) tall, and women were 1m 37cm (4ft 8in). Their skin was dark to light brown, their eyes and hair were black, and they had wide faces with hooked noses.

Nobles
The highest ranking noble was the Emperor. On the death of an Emperor the title usually passed to his brother, or if he did not have a brother then to a son or nephew.

Aztec nobles controlled the wealth of the empire. They owned land and governed the lives of the people who worked for them. Nobles lived in grand houses with servants. They paid no tax and could have many wives. Their children were well educated and girls had their marriages arranged with other wealthy families.

Commoners
The ordinary people formed the great mass of the Aztec population. They served in the army, worked in the fields, raised buildings and made objects for everyday and religious use. Commoners belonged to clans called 'calpulli', which means 'group of houses'. A 'calpulli' consisted of about 100 houses and was governed by an elected official.

Slaves were the lowest rank and were owned by their masters. They could be prisoners from tribes captured in battle or criminals serving a punishment for a crime.

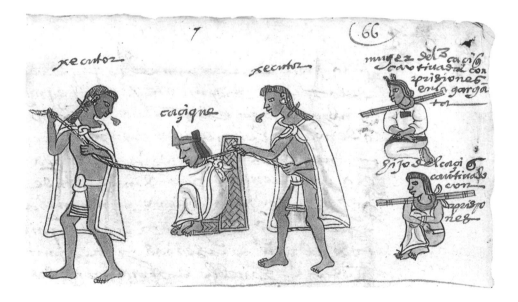

A picture from an Aztec codex (book) of a captured enemy leader and his family. As a prisoner he has had a rope placed around his neck, which is held by his Aztec captors. Behind him are his wife and daughter, both shown wearing slave collars.

Fact File

How did they dress?

Men wore loin-cloths. For commoners this was a piece of plain fabric wrapped around the waist. For nobles it was decorated with patterns and even edged with fur or precious feathers – signs of the wearer's wealth and status. Cloaks were also worn, held in place by a knot at the shoulder (the Aztecs did not use buttons or pins).

Women wore ankle-length skirts tied at the waist with a belt. Plain skirts were worn for everyday use, but for special occasions they put on skirts decorated with colourful designs. Women of the nobility wore long blouses over their skirts.

Commoners' clothes were made from fibres of the spiney-leaved maguey cactus. Cotton clothes were expensive because raw cotton had to be brought in from far away. Cotton was worn only by the nobles. The penalty for a commoner found wearing cotton clothes was death by stoning or strangulation.

An artist's reconstruction which shows how the Aztecs dressed. In the centre is a farmer wearing a simple, undecorated loin-cloth. He has been working in a field, gathering maize. The woman is wearing a long skirt and a simple slip-over blouse, both of which were made from coarse fibres from the maguey cactus. She is grinding the maize into flour. The man to the right is a noble, dressed in fine clothes made of cotton. Note that he is wearing sandals – most ordinary people went around barefoot.

Families and children

A child's rattle. Inside are beans which rattled when the object was shaken.

A picture from an Aztec codex (book) showing the birth of a child. To the left is the mother with her baby in its cot. To the right, a midwife washes the baby in a bowl of water placed on a rush mat. Footprints around the mat show the direction the midwife was expected to walk. To the right of the mat are three boys eating beans and maize. When ordered by the midwife they called out the baby's name. Above the mat are objects for a boy (spears and tools) and below are objects for a girl (a broom, a spindle and a work-basket).

Family life was important to the Aztecs. Boys married at about the age of 20, girls at about 15. Once married they became full members of their 'calpulli' or clan (see page 16), but as long as they stayed unmarried they did not have the full rights of adults, and they could not own land. The married couple set up home on one of the 'chinampas', or gardens. The man was the house-builder and farmer, and the woman cooked, tended animals and made clothes.

Children were especially important to the Aztecs and were seen as a gift from the gods. If the baby was a girl, her umbilical cord was buried near the hearth of the house. This represented the girl's life attached to the home. A boy's cord was dried and buried on a battlefield, showing that his life would be dedicated to warfare. A day associated with good fortune was chosen as the baby's naming day, after which boys ran to nearby houses calling the baby's name to the people inside.

As children grew up they were expected to learn from their parents. Girls learned how to weave and make clothes while boys were taught how to fish and farm the land. Disobedient children were punished. One form of punishment was to hold the child in the smoke of burning chilli peppers – the effects must have been similar to those from peeling onions! A punishment for boys was to be pricked with cactus spikes. Girls were given extra housework.

Grandparents and other elderly people were treated with respect. They were even allowed to get drunk on 'pulque', an alcoholic cactus juice drink. Drunkenness was usually considered an offence, but the rule was set aside for people over the age of 70.

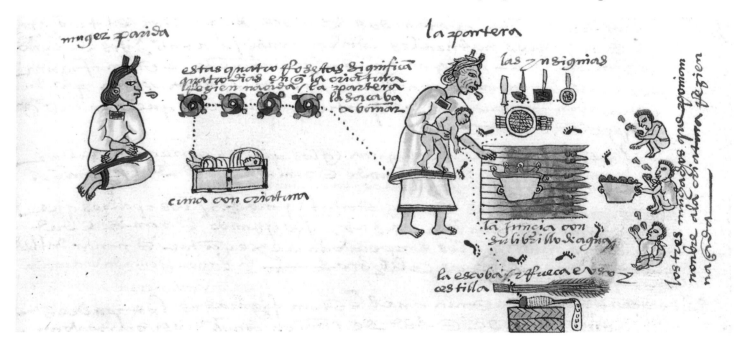

A page from an Aztec codex (book) showing children between the ages of 3 and 6 (1 blue dot = 1 year). At age 3, children receive half a cake of maize per day. At age 6, it was one-and-a-half cakes each. Boys' duties are shown to the left, girls' to the right. At age 4, boys fetch water; girls are shown the spindle. At age 5, boys carry light loads; girls begin to spin. At age 6, boys pick up left-overs at the market; girls spin cactus or cotton fibres. Boys were taught by their fathers and girls by their mothers.

Death was never far from the thoughts of adult Aztecs. To die in battle, or as a sacrifice to the gods, was considered a great honour, and the dead person's soul went straight to the Eastern Paradise (the Aztec version of heaven). The souls of people who died of old age or illness went to the Place of the Dead. This was another version of heaven, but to get there the soul had to travel on a long and difficult journey.

Going to school

A school education was an essential part of growing up, where children were turned into miniature adults, ready to face the demands of grown-up life. Children from noble families were sent to different schools from other children. Each 'calpulli', or clan, had a school for children of commoners in its territory. Boys and girls went to separate schools. At a boys' school instructors taught history, religion, good behaviour, music, singing and dancing. Boys were prepared for adult life and learned about fighting and weapons. Their time at school was deliberately harsh, in readiness for 'real life'. Boys from noble families were given a good education as they would one day become people with important duties. They learned subjects such as astrology, government, law, medicine and writing.

Girls could have the same education as boys, if their parents wished. But they were usually sent to temples and trained to become priestesses. Most left when it was time for them to marry, usually when they were 15 years old.

Law and order

Written records made by the Aztecs themselves, and by their Spanish observers, tell us about their laws.

Every aspect of Aztec life was governed by the law. For the Aztecs to be strong and successful they needed laws for people to follow – that way they could be sure of spotting trouble-makers and dealing with them.

A person accused of a crime was taken before a court where a group of judges decided whether he was guilty or not. The judges were specially chosen and were respected members of the community. In some cases the Emperor was in court to pronounce sentence. Court scribes recorded the case details and verdict.

The Aztecs believed in fair trials, but as the table to the right shows, they had harsh punishments for those found guilty.

A picture from an Aztec codex (book) showing four people executed for committing crimes. The dead man in the bottom right was a thief who has been stoned to death. The stones lie around him. Other forms of execution included strangulation, burning and cutting.

Breaking the law

Crime	Punishment
Adultery	Death
Commoner found wearing cotton clothes	Death
Cutting down a living tree	Death
Drunkenness	First offence: head shaved, house destroyed. Second offence: death
Handling stolen property	Sold into slavery
Kidnapping	Sold into slavery
Moving a field boundary	Death
Murder	Death
Selling sub-standard goods	Loss of property
Theft (major)	Death
Theft (minor)	Sold into slavery
Treason	Death, loss of property, destruction of land, children sold into slavery
Wearing sandals in the Emperor's palace	Death

Fact File

The Aztec calendar

Measuring time was a vital part of Aztec life. Two types of calendar were used. One measured 'real' time and the other was used to fix the times of religious festivals. This double system was used to work out the best time for planting crops (based on the real time calendar) and when to consult the gods (based on the religious calendar). In the real time calendar one year had 365 days divided into 18 months. Each month had 20 days. At the end of the year were 5 extra days which were bad-luck days when disasters were most likely to happen. In the religious calendar one year had 260 days divided into 13 months of 20 days each. The two calendars ran together and the same day in each fell at the same time once every 52 years. Because of this, Aztec time was divided into 52-year cycles – just like our own time is divided into 100-year cycles or centuries. Every day in the Aztec calendar belonged to a god. Days could be good or bad, depending on which god the day belonged to. The calendar was used to decide when to do certain duties. A child born on a bad day was given its name on a good day, to rule out harmful effects of the bad day.

The gigantic Stone of the Sun is 1.2 metres thick, 3.65 metres across and weighs 24 tonnes. It would have taken great skill and effort to carve and it was probably one of the most important objects in the capital, Tenochtitlan. The face at the centre is that of the Sun God, Tonatiuh. He is surrounded by signs from the Aztec calendar which tell the history of the world. The Aztecs believed their world could be divided into five ages. At the time of the Spanish conquest the Aztecs thought they were living in the fifth and final age – the previous four ages had been destroyed by rains, fires, hurricanes and jaguars. The fifth age was to be destroyed by earthquakes.

jaguars

doomsday, the end of the final age

hurricanes

fires

rains

20 signs in a circle, each one representing a different day of the religious month

Tonatiuh, the Sun God

Crafts of the Aztecs

Craftworkers were highly valued members of Aztec society. In Tenochtitlan, the Aztec capital, workers lived in their own parts of the great city. Each group of workers had its own patron god, and they guarded the secrets of their trade. Skills were passed down from parents to children ensuring they stayed within the family.

Objects of stone and metal were worn as jewellery. This man is wearing stone ear-plugs in his ear-lobes which have been stretched to take large objects. Through his nose is a gold nose-plug and through his lower lip is a gold lip-plug shaped like an eagle's head.

Feather objects
Clothes and other objects made from feathers were luxuries for the nobility. Feathers were collected by hunters who used nets to catch birds in the forests, such as the quetzal with its brilliant green feathers. Some birds with especially pretty plumage were kept in captivity for the sole purpose of providing feathers. Feathers could be coloured with dyes to make them even more beautiful. Weavers would then attach them to clothes, headresses, fans, armbands and ceremonial shields, as shown here.

An Aztec feather-worker using quetzal feathers to make a headress.

Fact File

Jewellery

Good jewellers were in great demand by the nobility. The most skilful jewellers came from the furthest parts of the Aztec empire to set up workshops in Tenochtitlan, where they made gold, silver and copper jewellery. Unfortunately we have found very little Aztec gold jewellery – most of what was made was melted down by the Spaniards.

Mosaic objects

Tiny stones of blue-green turquoise, black jet and yellow pyrites, together with crushed seashells, were glued in place to form mosaic objects. The two-headed dragon-like creature was probably a badge worn by an emperor or a priest. (The mosaic mask shown on the title page may have been used in religious ceremonies.)

Pottery

The potter's wheel was unknown to the Aztecs before the arrival of Spaniards in the 1500s. Before this time clay pots were made by hand, using techniques such as coil- and slab-building. The pots had thin walls and the finest examples were decorated with colourful designs of flowers, fish and other animals.

END OF THE AZTEC WORLD

The Aztecs are conquered

Hernán Cortés (1485–1547) shown in the fine armour of a Spanish military leader

After 200 years of conquests the Aztecs met people like no others they had seen before. Fair-skinned men with beards, wearing clothes of metal and riding strange animals came to Tenochtitlan. The year was 1519 and the strangers were from Spain.

Hernán Cortés, the leader of the Spaniards, arrived in Mexico in August 1519 in search of treasure. He had an army of 500 soldiers, 50 sailors, 200 Cuban bearers and some African servants. They arrived on board eleven ships and news of their landing was sent to Moctezuma II, the Aztec Emperor (see page 20), some 300 kilometres away. At first, Moctezuma thought they were gods, so he sent expensive gifts to make them feel welcome in his land.

Cortés saw the gifts as a clue to the riches ahead of him in Tenochtitlan. With his army, a young Indian woman called Doña Marina to act as interpreter and a group of friendly Indians, Cortés marched inland from the coast to the Aztec capital. The journey was hard and after 83 days Cortés reached Tenochtitlan. By then, only 350 of his own soldiers were still alive. But his small army was swelled by several thousand Indians who had joined forces with Cortés. These Indians were enemies of the Aztecs.

On 8 November 1519, Cortés met Moctezuma on a causeway that linked Tenochtitlan to the surrounding land. Cortés and his

The routes taken by Hernán Cortés

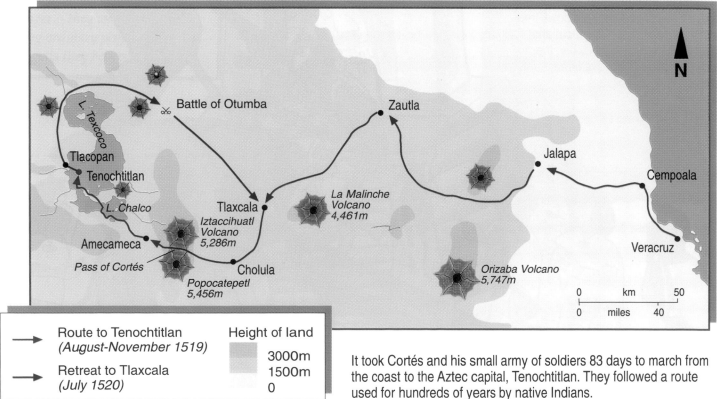

Route to Tenochtitlan (August–November 1519)

Retreat to Tlaxcala (July 1520)

Height of land
3000m
1500m
0

It took Cortés and his small army of soldiers 83 days to march from the coast to the Aztec capital, Tenochtitlan. They followed a route used for hundreds of years by native Indians.

An Aztec look-out sights the arrival of Cortés. This historic moment signalled the beginning of the end of the Aztec empire.

men were allowed to enter the city where they were treated as guests of honour. Soon they began to search for the gold they knew was there, and they took Moctezuma prisoner.

Between May and July 1520 the Aztecs rose up and fought the Spaniards. Many were killed on both sides, including Moctezuma, and the Spaniards fled from Tenochtitlan to Tlaxcala where they were given shelter by Indians who were enemies of the Aztecs. Life returned to normal in the Aztec city – but then smallpox broke out, a disease brought by the Spaniards which the Aztecs had no natural immunity to. With the Aztecs sick and weak, Cortés returned to Tenochtitlan in 1521. The city was besieged for 75 days and ended with a battle in the market-place.

Nearly 250,000 Aztecs died defending their city which was then looted and demolished by the Spaniards. The Aztec empire had fallen and the years of Spanish rule were about to begin.

▲ An iron treasure chest. Chests such as this were filled with plundered Aztec valuables and brought back to Europe.

▶ At first, Cortés was welcomed by the people he met. He was treated like a god. Here he is given a valuable jade necklace.

Fact File

Hernán Cortés

Hernán Cortés was born in 1485 in the Spanish town of Medellín. From an early age he learned the skills needed to be a soldier. In 1492, when Cortés was seven years old, Christopher Columbus reached the coast of America. Soon after, stories of a rich land in the west were told in Europe, particularly in Spain and Portugal. In 1504, when Cortés was 18, he sailed to America, hoping to return home a rich man. He landed in the West Indies where he settled for many years. When travellers showed him treasure from Mexico, Cortés planned to discover how rich that area was and so he set sail to Mexico for his encounter with the Aztecs in 1519 (see opposite). Cortés returned to Spain in 1540, where he died in 1547 aged 62. He wished to be buried in Mexico, but his wish only came true 20 years after his death when his bones were taken there.

Discovering the Aztecs

Every year there are archaeological excavations in Mexico City which uncover more evidence of the Aztecs. As modern buildings are demolished the archaeologists move in to look for signs that will tell them whether they should investigate further. A few scraps of pottery or some pieces of stone may turn up in a building site – clues that Aztec remains may not be far away.

When the archaeologists move in they carefully strip away all the modern layers. The deeper they dig the further back in time they go, until eventually they reach Aztec remains, which can be several metres below the modern ground level. The site is excavated, drawings are made and photographs are taken. As each new site is 'mapped', another piece in the jigsaw picture is filled in.

A giant stone head made by the Olmecs (see page 10) is displayed for all to see in the heart of Mexico City, reminding passers-by of their links with the past.

Beneath the streets of Mexico City lie the buried remains of Tenochtitlan, the Aztec capital.

Fact File

'Aztecs' today

Where did the Aztecs go to after their empire had fallen to the Spaniards? The answer is they didn't 'go' anywhere. Slowly they accepted the invaders and as more Spaniards arrived the Aztecs (and the other Indian tribes in Mexico, too) began to change their lifestyles.

Missionaries taught Christianity to the Aztecs, saying they must abandon their old gods The Aztecs learned to speak Spanish and this has become the language of present-day Mexico. The Aztecs and the Spaniards inter-married and their descendants are today's Mexicans. The site of their capital, Tenochtitlan, has become the capital of modern Mexico and one of the largest cities in the world.

Young descendants of the Aztecs.

At ancient sites throughout Mexico, archaeologists make records of the country's lost civilizations. Here, a team is making a tracing of the carvings on a stone column.

GLOSSARY AND PRONUNCIATION GUIDE

Aztec – 'The people whose face no one knows.' A group of Indians that lived in central Mexico during the two centuries before the Spanish conquest. They called themselves 'Mexica'.

Aztlan – 'The place of the herons.' According to legend, this was the place the Aztecs believed they originally came from.

ball-court – The playing ground for the ball game tlachtli.

calpulli – (kal-po-lee) The family clan to which a group of related Aztecs belonged.

causeway – A strip of dry land built over water.

chacmool – (chak-mool) A carved figure used to hold offerings from a sacrifice.

Chalchiuhtlicue – (chal-chee-uh-tlee-kwe) 'Our Lady of the Turquoise Skirt,' the goddess of water.

Chichen Itza – (chee-chen eet-sa) A large city in east Mexico lived in by the Maya people.

chinampas – (chee-nam-paz) Plots of farm land built in lake-beds. Often called 'floating gardens'.

chocolate – Beans from the cocoa tree were ground up and boiled with water to make a frothy drink of chocolate.

codex – A type of picture book which was an official, handwritten record. It was folded like a concertina.

Cortés, Hernán (1485–1547) – The leader of the Spanish army that conquered the Aztecs.

eagle warrior – A soldier of the nobility who wore a uniform covered with feathers and a helmet in the shape of an eagle's beak.

Huitzilopochtli – (weets-eel-oh-poach-tlee) 'The Hummingbird on the Left,' the god of war and the sun. He needed human blood and hearts for nourishment.

jade – a blue-green stone valued for precious objects.

jaguar warrior – A soldier of the nobility who wore a uniform made from ocelot skins. (An ocelot is a wild cat.)

Lake Texcoco – (tesh-ko-ko) The lake in which the Aztecs built their island city.

maguey cactus – A spiny leaved cactus for which the Aztecs had many uses.

Maya – A civilization of Mexico that flourished between the years 300 BC to AD 1500.

Mexico City – The modern capital of Mexico, built on the ruins of the Aztec capital city.

Mictlantecuhtli – (mic-tlan-tee-koo-tlee) 'Lord of the Realm of the Dead,' the god of the dead.

Moctezuma II – (mo-tek-zu-ma) The last great Aztec ruler. Reigned 1502–1520.

mosaic – Small pieces of stone, shell, eggshell or pottery that can be joined together to decorate an object or make a picture.

Nahuatl – (na-watl) The language of the Aztecs. It is still spoken in central Mexico today. Words such as chocolate and tomato came into the English language from Nahuatl.

obsidian – A shiny volcanic stone which looks like bottle-glass and was used for tools and weapon points.

Olmec – The first great civilization of Mexico. It flourished between the years 1200 to 400 BC.

patolli – (pa-to-lee) A gambling game played with pebbles and dried beans.

pulque – (pul-keh) An alcoholic drink made from the maguey cactus.

Quetzalcoatl – (ket-sal-ko-atl) 'Feathered Serpent,' the god of knowledge, priests and the wind. He was the creator god and was the most important and powerful of the Aztec gods. He was worshipped by other groups as well in Mexico, not just the Aztecs.

Tenochtitlan – (teh-noach-tee-tlan) 'Place of the prickly pear cactus fruit,' capital city of the Aztecs founded in 1325 and built on an island in Lake Texcoco.

Teotihuacan – (te-o-tee-wa-kan) 'Place where the gods were born,' a large and mysterious city in central Mexico that flourished between the years 100 BC to AD 750.

tlachtli – (tlach-tlee) A ball-court game played between teams using rubber balls.

Tlaloc – (tla-lok) 'Lord of the Sources of All Water,' the god of rain and fertility.

Toltec – A civilization of Mexico that flourished between the years 900 to 1150.

Tula – The Toltec capital city, plundered by the Aztecs.

Valley of Mexico – A large inland basin surrounded by volcanoes. Mexico City is located within this valley.

Xipe Totec – (shee-pe- to-tek) 'Our Flayed Lord,' the god of vegetation and springtime. His ceremony included the flaying and wearing of the skin of a sacrificial victim

INDEX

FURTHER READING

If you want to find out more about the Aztecs, these books will help

Aztec, Elizabeth Baquedano (Dorling Kindersley, 1993)
Life in the Time of Moctezuma and the Aztecs, Roy Burrell (Cherytree Books, 1992)
What Do We Know About The Aztecs? Joanna Defrates (Simon and Schuster, 1992)
The Expeditions of Cortés, Nigel Hunter (Wayland, 1990)
Aztecs, Fiona Macdonald (Oxford University Press, 1992)
The Aztecs, Tim Wood (Hamlyn, 1992)
History Detectives: The Aztecs, Philip Ardagh and Colin King (Macmillian, 1998)